REPUBLIC OF THE CONGO 2016 HUMAN RIGHTS REPORT

EXECUTIVE SUMMARY

The Republic of the Congo is a parliamentary republic in which the constitution, promulgated in November 2015, vests most decision-making authority and political power in the president and prime minister. In October 2015 citizens adopted the new constitution by a 94 percent vote, but the opposition and international community questioned the credibility of the referendum process and results. The new constitution changed previous maximum presidential term limits from two terms of seven years to three terms of five years and provided complete immunity to former presidents. On April 4, the Constitutional Court proclaimed the incumbent, Denis Sassou N'Guesso, winner of the March 20 presidential election with 60 percent of the vote and almost 69 percent voter turnout. Domestic nongovernmental organizations (NGOs), opposition candidates, foreign governments, and international organizations questioned the validity of the results and cited electoral irregularities. The government held the most recent legislative elections in 2012 for 137 of the national assembly's 139 seats. The African Union declared those elections free, fair, and credible, despite numerous irregularities. While the country has a multiparty political system, members of the president's Congolese Labor Party (PCT) and its allies held almost 90 percent of legislative seats, and PCT members occupied almost all senior government positions.

Civilian authorities generally maintained effective control over the security forces.

On April 4, gunfire and explosions in Brazzaville killed 17 persons, including three police officers, two civilians, and 12 attackers, according to the government. The violence displaced more than 17,000 persons, who fled their southern Brazzaville neighborhoods for safer parts of the city. The government blamed the Ninja/Nsiloulou, a former rebel group from the 1997-2003 civil war. Frederic Bintsamou, also known as Pastor Ntumi, the group's leader, denied responsibility. Many observers suggested the government coordinated the entire operation as a political distraction from the Constitutional Court's impending declaration of the presidential election results and to instill a climate of fear and intimidation. On April 5, the government launched security operations in the Pool region outside of Brazzaville to locate the Ninja/Nsiloulou and Pastor Ntumi. During the operation, thousands more in the Pool region were displaced from their homes. According to a June joint UN-Ministry of Social Affairs and Humanitarian Action humanitarian assessment report, hundreds of civilian homes were burned, with one documented death. The government initially denied access to the region to several international and local humanitarian assessment teams but later granted access with government escorts. A UN-led humanitarian assessment reported in June that more than 1,200 persons remained displaced in the Pool region, including 598 children. According to a December 9 statement by the Office of the UN High Commissioner for Refugees (UNHCR), at least 13,000 persons, including thousands of children, remained internally displaced. Periodic violent roadside attacks persisted in the Pool region following the initial operation, during which time rape and physical assaults were committed. The national government-affiliated newspaper reported approximately 100 deaths in the affected area since April 1. While the government blamed Ninja/Nsiloulou for these attacks, the identity and affiliation of the perpetrators were unconfirmed.

The most significant human rights problems included arbitrary or unlawful killings by security forces, arbitrary arrests and the holding of political prisoners, and torture and other cruel, inhuman, or degrading treatment or punishment of detainees by police.

Other major human rights abuses included: politically motivated disappearances; harsh detention conditions; lack of due judicial process; infringement of citizens' privacy rights; restrictions on freedoms of speech, press, assembly, and association; harsh treatment of undocumented immigrants; restrictions on the ability of citizens to change their government peacefully; restrictions on the activities of opposition political groups; corruption on the part of officials and lack of transparency; discrimination against women; sexual and gender-based violence, including domestic violence, child abuse, and early marriage; trafficking in persons; lack of access for persons with disabilities; societal discrimination on the basis of ethnicity, particularly toward indigenous persons; discrimination based on nationality, particularly toward individuals from the Democratic Republic of the Congo (DRC), Central African Republic (CAR), and Rwanda; discrimination based on sexual orientation and HIV/AIDS status; and child labor.

The government seldom took steps to prosecute or punish officials who committed abuses, whether in the security services or elsewhere in the government, and official impunity was a problem.

Section 1. Respect for the Integrity of the Person, Including Freedom from:

a. Arbitrary Deprivation of Life and other Unlawful or Politically Motivated Killings

There were reports the government or its agents committed arbitrary or unlawful killings.

Journalists and local human rights activists presented evidence of four deaths resulting from torture. According to a joint report from three local human rights organizations, on February 26, police arrested Olgane Nioko Ngambou for an alleged robbery in Owando, in the central Cuvette region. Sergeant Cedric Akoul severely beat Ngambou while in custody at the Owando Police Station, and he died from internal hemorrhaging of the liver and kidneys on February 27 after officials transferred him to the Central Hospital in Brazzaville for urgent medical treatment. Other deaths reported included Steve Malonga, arrested March 25 and detained at the Chacona Police Station; Yeutcheu Faustin Aime, a Cameroonian citizen arrested in June in Pointe-Noire and detained at the Tie Tie Police Station; and Fabrice Oyakou, arrested June 15 and detained at the Poto Poto Police Station in Brazzaville.

According to multiple NGO reports, on July 21, police shot and killed Mankou Albert, Aikon Apollinaire, and Nsihou Paul, civilians belonging to a community night watch patrol in the Raffinerie neighborhood of Pointe-Noire. Police intercepted the men, who were armed with machetes and whistles, and according to eyewitnesses, questioned the men at gunpoint about their activities and moments later shot and killed them. On July 21, Itoua Poto, police chief of Pointe-Noire, stated the victims belonged to a militia and that police who shot them had committed no error.

Vigilante justice and abuse of power by police were problems. For example, on April 26, Police Brigadier General Mba Ferdinand, in the southern town of Madingou, shot Ngembo Olombi Mignon, age 15, at his house, after learning that Mignon had harmed a young neighbor girl. Mignon died later that night in a hospital. In response to his death, youth set fire to the police station in Madingou.

Human rights NGOs reported at least seven deaths resulting from abuse in prisons and pretrial detention centers (see sections 1.c. and 1.g.).

b. Disappearance

There were numerous credible reports of politically motivated disappearances. For example, independent media and local human rights NGOs reported the disappearance of political opposition members Marien Michel Ehouango Madzimba, arrested on April 30, and Rodiguez Bazembe, arrested on June 17.

Additionally, there were several reports of night raids and daytime state-sponsored kidnappings of opposition supporters, after which family members were unable to find any information about the victims' welfare and whereabouts.

Police detained minor children, who subsequently disappeared (see section 1.c.).

c. Torture and Other Cruel, Inhuman, or Degrading Treatment or Punishment

The constitution prohibits torture, and the law contains a general prohibition against assault and battery, but there is no legal framework specifically banning torture under the criminal code. There were widespread reports of cases of government-led torture and other cruel, inhuman, and degrading treatment.

A human rights NGO reported that in December 2015 sergeants Sabin Assima Atsouama and Morgan Atsouama allegedly tortured Rigobert Okuya. According to Okuya, he was strapped down on a table for hours, severely beaten, temporarily paralyzed by a stun gun, and sodomized with a metal rod.

In September, NGOs and media reported the arrest and torture of Augustin Kala Kala, a campaign official belonging to the Convention for Action, Democracy, and Development, an opposition political group. According to Kala Kala's wife, more than a dozen armed and hooded men belonging to government security forces arrested Kala Kala at his residence in Brazzaville during the middle of the night on September 28. Police took him to a local intelligence police station where intelligence police subjected him to electric shock and beatings over a period of two weeks. On October 15, Kala Kala was found barely conscious in front of a morgue in Brazzaville and given medical attention.

According to human rights NGOs and social media reports, on November 12, armed and hooded men belonging to government security forces abducted Jugal Mayangui, a sergeant in the military, from his home in Brazzaville. According to Mayangui, he was muzzled, burned, molested, and subjected to severe beatings and accused of being an accomplice to Pastor Ntumi. The abductors released him on November 20, and he was taken to a hospital for treatment.

On December 21, prison authorities brought Roland Gambou, the younger brother of opposition candidate Okombi Salissa, to the hospital where he died of unspecified causes after more than four months of detention.

Other cruel, inhuman, or degrading treatment or punishment regularly took place. Human rights NGOs reported authorities regularly beat numerous detainees while in custody. On July 28, Jean Ngouabi, detained in the Brazzaville Prison, reported to a human rights NGO that police arrested him on March 25 and subsequently subjected him to severe beatings over the next 27 days. Because of the blows to his head, he developed blood clots, and according to medical records provided by his lawyer, lost all vision in his right eye and some vision in his left eye. The government denied responsibility, claiming a pre-existing health condition caused his vision loss. According to human rights NGOs, many detainees developed chronic medical problems such as organ damage and paralysis due to lack of proper medical care.

Police frequently required detainees to pay for protection or risk beatings. NGOs reported authorities generally ignored allegations of prisoner mistreatment.

Rape and sexual abuse by government agents occurred. In June a joint UN-Congolese government report cited indications that sexual violence toward women and teenage girls corresponded to the timing of security operations in the southern Pool region. Human rights NGOs reported multiple instances of rape and sexual abuse by police, particularly of prostitutes and gay men.

Although prostitution is legal, there were reports of police arresting prostitutes, including gay men, for alleged illegal activity; police then threatened or committed rape if the detainees did not pay a bribe for release.

The United Nations reported that during the year (through December 20), it received nine allegations of sexual exploitation and abuse against Republic of the Congo peacekeepers deployed to the UN Multidimensional Integrated Stabilization Mission in the CAR. These include three alleged incidents occurring in 2016, five in 2015, and one for which the date of the alleged incident was unknown. Investigations into these nine allegations by the United Nations and the Government of the Republic of the Congo were pending at year's end.

Conflict abuses during international peacekeeping missions allegedly took place. On June 7, Human Rights Watch (HRW) reported that Congolese peacekeepers in Boali, CAR, killed 18 civilians between December 2013 and June 2015. HRW made these allegations based on a grave exhumed near a peacekeeping base on February 16, in which the remains of 12 bodies matched the identities of missing persons from March 2014. On June 8, Minister of Justice Pierre Mabiala, responded that the soldiers in question would face justice by the end of the year. At year's end the investigation was still pending.

Prison and Detention Center Conditions

Prison and detention center conditions were harsh and life threatening due to inadequate sanitary conditions, gross overcrowding, and a severe deficit of medical and psychological care.

Authorities generally maintained separate areas within facilities for minors, women, and men in Brazzaville and Pointe-Noire, however, there were times when 16-17-year-old males were held in the same area as women in Pointe Noire. In Brazzaville, while these areas were separate, they were sometimes easily accessible with no locked entryways. In the other 10 prisons, authorities sometimes held juvenile detainees with adult prisoners.

<u>Physical Conditions</u>: As of September 8, there were approximately 1,200 inmates in the country's two largest prisons--Brazzaville and Pointe-Noire prisons. A government source estimated 60 percent of inmates awaited trial, but according to an NGO, that total was closer to 75 percent. As of November 30, the Brazzaville Prison, built in 1943 to accommodate 150 prisoners, held more than 800 inmates, including women and minors. It had only 110 beds and 24 showers and toilets. The Pointe-Noire Prison, built in 1934 to hold up to 75 inmates, held an estimated 400, including 60 foreign nationals, more than half of whom were from the DRC. Police stations regularly housed individuals in their limited incarceration facilities beyond the maximum statutory holding period of 72 hours. In addition to these official prisons, the government's intelligence and security services operated several secret detention centers and security prisons, which were inaccessible for inspection.

Prison conditions for women were better than those for men in all 12 prisons. There was less crowding in the women's cells than in those for men. Authorities held pretrial detainees with convicted prisoners. In Brazzaville authorities housed and treated prisoners with illnesses in one area but allowed them to interact with other inmates.

In Brazzaville prison conditions for wealthy or well connected prisoners generally were better than conditions for others.

There were several reported deaths resulting from abuse, neglect, and overcrowding in prisons and pretrial detention centers (see section 1.a.). For example, an NGO reported that in February Michel Nganda Manenga, incarcerated since 2013, died from malnutrition in the Ouesso Jail in Sangha Department. According to the same NGO, six inmates died in the Brazzaville Prison in July for reasons prison administrators did not disclose.

On June 11, NGOs reported the forced disappearance of Mayama Saint Etude, age 11. Police arrested Etude for alleged theft and detained him in a special unit called the Banditry Repression Group at the Ouenze Mandzandza Police Station in Brazzaville. They denied his parents' repeated requests for access to visit him in detention. On June 29, the parents received an anonymous tip that their son had died in detention shortly after his arrest. On July 4, Etude's parents met with the police commissioner of the police station, who denied Etude had ever been arrested or detained.

On December 29, an attempted prison break in Brazzaville led to the death of three individuals--a gendarme, a prisoner, and a passerby, according to the government.

In Brazzaville most inmates slept on the floor on cardboard or thin mattresses in small, overcrowded cells that exposed them to disease. The prisons lacked ventilation and had poorly maintained lighting with wiring protruding from the walls. In Brazzaville stagnant water with trash lined the interior space of one holding area. In Pointe-Noire water regularly backed into prisoners' cells. Basic and emergency medical care was limited. Medical personnel at a Brazzaville prison cited tuberculosis, dysentery, malaria, and HIV as the most common maladies affecting prisoners. Authorities did not provide prisoners with HIV/AIDS with specialized medical care, nor were HIV tests available in prisons. Authorities took pregnant women to hospitals to give birth, and authorities sometimes allowed them to breastfeed their infants in prison. Access to social services personnel was severely limited due to insufficient staffing, overcrowding, and stigmatization of mental health issues.

Prison inmates reportedly received, on average, two daily meals consisting of rice, bread, and fish or meat. Authorities permitted women to cook over small fires built on the ground in a shared recreational space. The Pointe-Noire Prison occasionally had running water. All of the prisons supplied potable water to inmates in buckets.

<u>Administration</u>: Recordkeeping in the penitentiary system was inadequate. Despite having the necessary computer equipment in Brazzaville and Pointe-Noire, prison officials continued to rely mostly on a noncomputerized system, citing a lack of internet access, resources, and training.

Access to prisoners generally required a communication permit from a judge. The permit allowed visitors to spend five to 15 minutes with a prisoner, although authorities usually did not strictly enforce this limit. In most cases visits took place either in a crowded open area or in a small room with one extended table where approximately 10 detainees sat at a time. A new permit is technically required for each visit, but families were often able to return for multiple visits on one permit. Since many prisoners' families lived far away, visits often were infrequent because of the financial hardship of travel.

Prison rules provide for prisoners and detainees to submit complaints to judicial authorities without censorship, but officials did not respect this right. Authorities did not investigate credible allegations of inhuman conditions brought to them by NGOs and detainees' families.

<u>Independent Monitoring</u>: The government provided domestic and international human rights groups with limited access to prisons and detention centers. Observers generally considered the primary local NGO focused on prison conditions independent; authorities, however, denied it access to the interior of several different prisons on multiple occasions throughout the year.

Throughout the year human rights NGOs that monitored detention conditions requested letters of permission from the Ministry of Justice to visit prisons. Their repeated requests went unanswered, so prisons in Djambala and Brazzaville, and police detention stations in Sembe and Sangha, continued to refuse these NGOs access.

Representatives of religiously affiliated charitable organizations visited prisons and detention centers for charitable work and religious counseling. Authorities granted diplomatic missions access to both prisons and police jails to provide consular assistance to their citizens and for general inspection.

d. Arbitrary Arrest or Detention

The constitution and law prohibit arbitrary arrest and detention. Nevertheless, arbitrary arrest continued to be a widespread problem. Local NGOs reported hundreds of arbitrary detentions in the period leading up to and after the March 20 presidential election, although more-definitive evidence was available for only 88 cases during the year.

Role of the Police and Security Apparatus

Security forces consist of the police, gendarmerie, and military. Police and the gendarmerie are responsible for maintaining internal order, with police primarily operating in cities and the gendarmerie mainly in other areas. Military forces are responsible for territorial security, but some units also have domestic security responsibilities. For example, the specialized Republican Guard battalion is charged with the protection of the president, government buildings, and diplomatic missions. The Ministry of Defense oversees the military and gendarmerie, and the Ministry of the Interior and Decentralization oversees the police.

A civilian police unit under the Ministry of Interior and Decentralization is responsible for patrolling the borders. Separately, a military police unit reports to the Ministry of Defense and is composed of military and police officers responsible for investigating professional misconduct by members of any of the security forces.

Civilian authorities generally maintained effective control over the security forces; however, there were members of the security forces who acted independently of civilian authority, committed abuses, and engaged in malfeasance. The law charges both the military police and the Office of the Inspector General of Police with investigating reports of misconduct by security forces.

In March a Brazzaville court sentenced police officer Dany Mayala to five years in prison for committing "intentional injury" to a detainee at the Diata Police Station in 2013.

The government-established Human Rights Commission (HRC) receives reports from the public of security force abuses, but it was ineffective and did not meet during the year.

Impunity for members of the security forces remained widespread. On April 4, security forces were mostly professional and restrained during the aftermath of gunfire in Brazzaville that displaced thousands of persons. There were, however, several reports of security force members robbing displaced persons of their valuable possessions, such as cell phones, and demanding bribes at checkpoints within the city. Additionally, their commanders and other government officials often ordered them to commit human rights abuses, such as preventing freedom of movement throughout the country during the presidential campaign period in March.

Arrest Procedures and Treatment of Detainees

The constitution and law require that a duly authorized official issue warrants before making arrests, a person be apprehended openly, a lawyer be present during initial questioning, and detainees be brought before a judge within three days and either charged or released within four months. The government habitually violated these provisions. There is a bail system, but with 70 percent of the population living in poverty, most detainees could not afford to post bail. There is an option for provisional release, but officials usually denied these requests, even for detainees with serious medical conditions. Authorities sometimes informed detainees of charges against them at the time of arrest, but filing of formal charges often took at least one week. Authorities often arrested detainees secretly and without judicial authorization and sometimes detained suspects incommunicado or put them under de facto house arrest. Police at times held persons for six months or longer before filing charges due to the political nature of the cases or administrative errors. Observers attributed most administrative delays to lack of staff in the Ministry of Justice and the court system. Family members sometimes received prompt access to detainees but often only after payment of bribes. The law requires authorities to provide lawyers to indigent detainees facing criminal charges at government expense, but this usually did not occur.

The penal code states authorities may hold a detainee for a maximum of 48 to 72 hours in a police jail before an attorney general reviews the case. Thereafter, a decision must be made either to release or to transfer the individual to a prison for pretrial detention. Authorities generally did not observe the 72-hour maximum and frequently held detainees for several weeks before an attorney general freed or transferred them to a prison to await trial. The criminal code states that a defendant or accused person may apply for provisional release at any point during his or her detention, from either an investigating judge or a trial court, depending on the type of case. The law states that provisional release should generally be granted, provided that the judicial investigation is sufficiently advanced, that the accused does not pose a risk of subornation of witnesses, and does not pose a threat of disturbance to public order caused by the offense initially alleged; however, this law was not respected in practice.

<u>Arbitrary Arrest</u>: Arbitrary and false arrests continued to occur. Authorities arrested more than eight persons belonging to opposition political parties or suspected of supporting the opposition. According to eyewitnesses and local human rights NGOs, police conducted secret arrests, often at night, at the homes of opposition supporters. Independent media and local NGOS published lists of hundreds of names of individuals arrested between January and July.

<u>Pretrial Detention</u>: The penal code sets a maximum of four months in pretrial detention, which may be extended an additional two months with judicial approval; thereafter detainees must be released pending their court hearings. Authorities did not respect this limit, arguing that the two-month extension is renewable. Between 60 and 75 percent of detainees in the prisons were pretrial detainees. Prison authorities stated the average provisional detention for noncriminal cases lasted one to three months and for criminal cases at least 12 months. Human rights activists, however, stated the average was much longer, commonly exceeding a year, and sometimes exceeding the maximum sentence for the alleged crime.

For example, in November 2015 authorities arrested Paulin Makaya, president of the opposition United for Congo Party for "incitement to public disorder" for organizing and participating in an unauthorized demonstration in October 2015 against the constitutional referendum. Makaya remained in pretrial detention for six months before his trial began on June 13.

Lengthy pretrial detentions were primarily due to the judicial system's lack of capacity and political will. The penal code defines three levels of crime: the misdemeanor (punishable by less than one year in jail), the delict (punishable by one to five years in jail), and the felony (punishable by more than five years in jail). Criminal courts try misdemeanor and delict cases regularly. The judicial system, however, suffered from a serious backlog of felony cases. By law criminal courts must hear felony cases four times per year. This was not possible because the ministry received funding irregularly for processing the more expensive and legally complex felony cases.

<u>Detainee's Ability to Challenge Lawfulness of Detention before a Court</u>: The constitution and law prohibit arbitrary arrest, arbitrary detention, and false arrest, and provide detainees the right to challenge the legal basis of their detention before a competent judge or authority. If an investigating judge determines a detainee to be innocent, his or her release is promptly ordered, and he or she is entitled to file suit against the government for miscarriage of justice with the Administrative Court. The government generally did not observe the law. Local human rights

NGOs reported numerous occasions when officials denied detainees in Brazzaville the right to challenge their detention.

e. Denial of Fair Public Trial

Although the constitution and law provide for an independent judiciary, the judiciary continued to be overburdened, underfunded, and subject to political influence and corruption. Authorities generally abided by court orders; however, judges did not always issue direct court orders against accused authorities.

In rural areas traditional courts continued to handle many local disputes, particularly property, inheritance, and witchcraft cases, and domestic conflicts that could not be resolved within the family.

Trial Procedures

The constitution provides for the right to a fair trial presided over by an independent judiciary, but authorities did not always respect this right. In 2011 the Ministry of Justice began to decentralize the trial process. Appeals courts existed in five departments--Brazzaville, Pointe-Noire, Dolisie, Owando, and Ouesso--and each had authority to try felony cases brought within its jurisdiction.

Defendants have the right to be informed promptly and in detail of the charges, with free interpretation as necessary. Defendants have a right to a fair and public trial in all criminal cases and felony cases. Defendants in all criminal trials have the right to be present at their trials and to consult with an attorney in a timely manner, although this did not always occur. The law obligates the government to provide legal assistance to any indigent defendant facing serious criminal charges, but such legal assistance was not always available because the government did not generally pay for public defenders.

Defendants have the right to adequate time and facilities to prepare a defense. The defense has the right to access government-held evidence. Defendants also have the right to confront or question accusers and witnesses against them and present witnesses and evidence on their own behalf. Defendants have the right not to be compelled to testify or confess guilt and have the right to appeal. The law extends these rights to all citizens, and the government generally abided by these provisions, except in highly politicized cases.

Political Prisoners and Detainees

During the year NGOs reported authorities held 131 political prisoners, who had publicly opposed another term for the incumbent president; some cases dated back to August 2015. A total of 88 others were detained since January. For example, authorities arrested senior campaign officials of opposition presidential candidates the week following the March 20 presidential election, including Jean Ngouabi, Jacques Banagandzala, Anatole Limbongo Ngoka, Christine Moyen, Dieudonne Dhird, Raymond Ebonga, and Serge Blanchard Oba. In addition, the government put several opposition figures under house arrest or had their houses surrounded by security forces. On April 6, Guy Brice Parfait Kolelas, the declared runner-up in the presidential election, reported his house was under police surveillance for several weeks. Security forces reportedly surrounded the house of opposition candidate Okombi Salissa; the candidate's actual whereabouts were unknown. From April 13 until April 20, security forces surrounded the private residence of candidate Claudine Munari. Security forces also surrounded the residence of retired general Jean-Marie Michel Mokoko, the candidate who came in third officially with 14 percent of vote. On June 14, authorities arrested Mokoko on charges of posing a threat to national security and possession of weapons of war. He faced an additional charge on August 17 of disturbing public order. On August 18, authorities denied him provisional release and as of year's end, he remained in detention in Brazzaville.

The government permitted limited access to political prisoners by international human rights and humanitarian organizations, and diplomatic missions.

Civil Judicial Procedures and Remedies

In contrast to felony courts, civil courts reviewed cases on a regular basis throughout the year. Civil courts experienced long delays--although shorter than felony courts--but were considered functional. Individuals may file a lawsuit in court on civil matters related to human rights, including seeking damages for or cessation of a human rights violation. The public, however, generally lacked confidence in the judicial system's ability to address human rights problems.

f. Arbitrary or Unlawful Interference with Privacy, Family, Home, or Correspondence

The constitution and law prohibit such actions; the government, however, did not always respect these prohibitions.

There were reports government authorities entered homes without judicial or other appropriate authorization; monitored private communications without appropriate legal authority, including e-mail, text messaging, or other digital communications intended to remain private; monitored private movements; accessed personal data and employed informer systems.

For example, on March 31, police issued fines of 500,000 CFA francs, ($856) under threat of permanent closure to shop owners who had closed during a March 29 general stay-at-home strike called by the opposition to protest the provisional results of the presidential election, announced on March 22.

Between January and June, there were dozens of reports police entered homes without judicial authorization, often in the middle of the night, to conduct searches and arrests.

g. Abuses in Internal Conflict

Killings: Multiple sources reported at least one death resulting from violence on April 4 in Brazzaville; in October the government asserted that militiamen called Ninja/Nsiloulou killed 17 persons. A UN report cited one civilian death resulting from a security force operation launched on April 5 in the southern Pool region as well as multiple injuries to civilians fleeing their homes. The government reported that 14 persons, including 11 civilians, died during a September 30 attack on a freight train by Ninja militia in the southern Pool region.

Physical Abuse, Punishment, and Torture: A joint UN-Congolese government report cited an increase in indicators of sexual violence toward women and teenage girls corresponding to security operations in the southern Pool region.

Other Conflict-related Abuse: From April 5 to May 6, the government deliberately restricted the passage of relief supplies, food, drinking water, and medical aid by impartial international humanitarian organizations like the United Nations. On April 6, a government helicopter strafed an empty elementary school in the village of Vindza and medical centers in Mayama in the southern Pool region. The government-led security operation forcibly displaced thousands of civilians for reasons other than military necessity. A UN humanitarian report said the government systematically burned and destroyed approximately half of homes in some villages in the region. According to NGOs, authorities ordered villagers in the region to flee the area, obligating them to walk many miles to larger urban areas. NGOs also reported a series of lootings by security forces in the region.

Section 2. Respect for Civil Liberties, Including:

a. Freedom of Speech and Press

The constitution and law provide for freedom of speech and press, but authorities often restricted these rights for those supporting political opponents. The government increased its media restrictions and journalist intimidation by closing one newspaper and radio station, disrupting the local retransmission signals of international media, and arresting three journalists.

Freedom of Speech and Expression: Individuals could criticize the government publicly or privately on relatively minor issues but risked reprisal, including arrest and prolonged detention, if they named high-level officials while criticizing government policies. The constitution provides for freedom of expression in all forms of communication and prohibits censorship. The constitution, however, criminalizes speech that incites ethnic hatred, violence, or civil war and makes it punishable by no less than five years in jail. It also criminalizes any act or event that promotes racism or xenophobia. Authorities cited this law at least once during the year in the context of closing the satirical newspaper *Sel Piment*.

Press and Media Freedoms: There was one official state-owned newspaper, *La Nouvelle Republique*, which published irregularly, and approximately 100 private publications, most of which were closely aligned with the government; others occasionally criticized the government. One daily newspaper that received government funding and a semiweekly newspaper founded by the Catholic Church were the only publications with circulation outside Brazzaville.

Most citizens obtained their news from local retransmission of international media and local radio or television stations. Approximately 95 radio stations, three of which were government-owned, and 26 television stations, two of which were government-owned, operated with limited coverage throughout the country. Tele-Congo and Radio Congo, both government-owned, were the only stations with nationwide coverage. Tele-Congo did not cover many events that took a critical view of the government. The majority of radio and television stations not owned by the government had low bandwidth, did not reach large parts of the country, and were owned by politicians or members of the government. Satellite television services were available for the few who could afford them.

By law media outlets are required to register with the Superior Council for Liberty of Communication (CSLC), the independent media regulatory body whose director is selected by the president. According to its charter, the CSLC is authorized to impose financial sanctions on any media outlet that violates media regulations. The law requires journalists to have a press card issued by the CSLC. To get a press card, journalists must provide evidence of their training or degree in journalism, a criminal background check, and a residency card and also have their names submitted by their former employer. Freelance journalists must apply through a CSLC-registered entity. Authorities may subject journalists without press cards to arrest and imprisonment, although according to freelance journalists, authorities did not enforce the law, and many journalists operated freely without a press card.

Government journalists generally were not independent, and the majority of journalists and editors practiced self-censorship and promoted the editorial views of media owners, most of whom were current or former government officials. Newspapers occasionally published open letters written by government opponents.

<u>Violence and Harassment</u>: There were multiple reports of direct and indirect intimidation by the government.

For example, on February 9, Alphonse Ndongo, a journalist with the online news website *Congo Jeune Afrique Economy*, reported several men in civilian clothes beat him at Maya Maya airport in Brazzaville while waiting for presidential candidate General Jean Michel Mokoko (ret.) to arrive. Reporters from DRTV, a local private television station, also reported that police stripped them of their property while they attempted to cover the same event. Eyewitnesses reported police fired tear gas and used physical force to disperse the remaining crowd of journalists and onlookers. Thugs from busses with no license plates threw large rocks at the candidate and the crowd.

On March 23, following the presidential election, unknown assailants attacked and robbed three international journalists who were departing a press conference at the campaign headquarters of Mokoko in Brazzaville.

On March 30, police arrested Franck Mboungou, managing editor of local newspaper *Pole Pole*, a publication critical of the government. On April 11, police arrested journalist Guy Milex Mboundzi, reportedly for his attempted coverage of the opposition.

The director of the Talassa Media Group alleged that on July 22, authorities searched his house without judicial authorization under the pretext of searching for weapons and ammunition.

Additional reports of alleged intimidation included the following: police use of nonlethal force against journalists attempting to report on sensitive events; attempts to prevent journalists sympathetic to the opposition from traveling internationally; telephone calls from official and anonymous persons warning journalists not to use footage of politically sensitive events; removing journalists from positions of leadership for covering opposition candidates and platforms during the campaign period; administrative closures and withdrawal of operating licenses of private news organizations; and pressure on news outlets not to run certain stories or footage.

Censorship or Content Restrictions: On January 22, the CSLC suspended *Sel Piment* for inciting tribal hatred and undermining national cohesion.

Several newspaper suspensions imposed since 2013 continued, including those of *Le Nouveau Regard*, *La Verite*, and *La Voix du Peuple*. Private newspapers and websites affiliated with government officials received no sanctions for falsehoods they published.

Most independent and government-employed journalists continued to practice self-censorship. There were no reports the government revoked journalists' accreditations if their reporting reflected adversely on the government's image, but journalists reported a fear of termination from their government positions for doing so.

Libel/Slander Laws: The press law provides for monetary penalties and suspension of a publication's permission to print for defamation and incitement to violence.

National Security: On several occasions throughout the year, journalists reported authorities cited laws protecting national security to restrict media distribution of material that criticized government policies or public officials. For example, on April 10, citing national security concerns, police blocked journalists from Radio France International from travelling to Kinkala to cover government-initiated security operations in the southern Pool region.

Internet Freedom

The government disrupted communication networks and internet access used to enable persons to assemble peacefully prior to elections or planned demonstrations during the year. For example, on March 20, the government cut most internet links, fiber optic networks, Short Message Service (SMS) services, and cellular voice service, effectively preventing the transmission of parallel vote counts by candidate representatives throughout the country. Authorities intermittently restored voice service on March 24, but internet and SMS services remained almost completely unavailable until March 26.

According to the International Telecommunication Union, approximately 7 percent of individuals used the internet in 2015.

Academic Freedom and Cultural Events

In December 2015 authorities banned actor, director, and playwright Dieudonne Niangouna from participating in an international theater festival in Brazzaville after he published an open letter criticizing the president for having held a referendum on a new constitution that allowed him to run for president again.

Self-censorship was common in academia and at cultural events, especially in universities, where there was little room for public discourse on politically sensitive topics. University-level professors were not always intellectually independent, since many held second jobs as close advisors to government officials.

b. Freedom of Peaceful Assembly and Association

Freedom of Assembly

The constitution and law provide for freedom of assembly; however, the government did not respect this right during the campaign period prior to the March 20 presidential election. For example, officials temporarily blocked at least two opposition candidates from visiting the northern region of Likouala during the official campaign period.

The government required groups that wished to hold public assemblies to seek authorization from the Ministry of Interior and Decentralization and appropriate local officials. Both the ministry and local officials sometimes withheld authorization for meetings they claimed might threaten public order. They also created unnecessary obstacles to gaining authorization and called police to disperse meetings they claimed had not received proper authorization.

On June 16, authorities stopped the Initiative for Democracy in Congo-Republican Front for the Respect of Constitutional Order and Democratic Change (IDC-FROCAD), a coalition regrouping most major opposition figures, from holding a press conference in Brazzaville to condemn the incarceration of opposition leader and candidate General Jean-Marie Michel Mokoko.

Freedom of Association

The constitution and law provide for freedom of association, and the government sometimes respected this right. Political, social, or economic groups or associations were required to register with the Ministry of Interior and Decentralization. Authorities sometimes subjected registration to political influence. According to a local NGO, groups that spoke openly against the government encountered overt or veiled threats and found the registration process more time-consuming.

Between February and April, members of Ras-le-Bol ("enough is enough")--a political youth activist group whose members had been arrested for politically oriented activities in the past--reported numerous direct threats from police to stop their activities. Police officially summoned two of the group's members. Other members reported police harassed their families and friends to ascertain their whereabouts.

c. Freedom of Religion

See the Department of State's *International Religious Freedom Report* at www.state.gov/religiousfreedomreport/.

d. Freedom of Movement, Internally Displaced Persons, Protection of Refugees, and Stateless Persons

The constitution and law provide for freedom of internal movement, foreign travel, emigration, and repatriation. The government generally respected these rights for refugees and asylum seekers, but not for undocumented immigrants from the DRC in the country's larger cities.

The government usually cooperated with UNHCR and other humanitarian organizations in providing protection and assistance to internally displaced persons, refugees, returning refugees, asylum seekers, stateless persons, and other persons of concern.

<u>Abuse of Migrants, Refugees, and Stateless Persons</u>: Authorities harassed and arbitrarily arrested refugees on a regular basis, forcing them to pay small bribes to avoid arrest or obtain release. Police, specifically the intelligence police, arrested at least 145 refugees during the year, including 105 in Brazzaville and 40 in the northern town of Betou. In 27 cases police cited irregular immigration as the cause for arrest, despite the refugees carrying valid identification cards indicating refugee status. For example, police regularly arrested CAR refugees, claiming they no longer had refugee status since the war in CAR had ended. Dozens of refugees reported that police used physical violence against them during their arrest and detention. On three separate occasions, refugees reported violent physical harassment by police and military members who demanded money from them outside a detention center.

On March 11, intelligence police arrested without charge Rwandan refugee Bonfiface Uzaribara; as of October 20, he remained in detention. Authorities denied human rights organizations, UNHCR, and Uzaribara's family and lawyer access to visit him in detention.

UNHCR reported 28 cases of rape from January through September, 19 of which involved rape of a minor and 15 of which occurred frequently at a refugee camp in Betou. Soldiers allegedly committed two of the rapes in the northern Likuala region. Rape and sexual abuse commonly occurred during the initial flight; many women and girls engaged in survival sex in exchange for protection, material goods, or money. Women often remained with abusive partners who offered protection during the flight and subsequently reported domestic abuse and marital rape. The vast majority of gender-based violence incidents went unreported because complaints could take three or more years before courts examined them. Families of victims often preferred settlements through traditional justice mechanisms of negotiating directly with the perpetrators. UNHCR's protection officers and medical partners provided medical, psychosocial, and legal assistance to victims of gender-based violence, including rape. During the year there was a national shortage of rape kits and HIV testing to respond to victims. Refugees had equal access to community health centers and hospitals but reported discriminatory treatment at some hospitals, including insults by medical personnel and not being treated in priority order relative to their medical condition. Refugees had equal legal recourse for criminal complaints (for example, rape) and civil disputes.

Foreign Travel: The law provides for freedom of internal movement, foreign travel, emigration, and repatriation, but the government repeatedly violated these rights, especially for opposition politicians and supporters attempting to depart the country.

By law all citizens are eligible for a national passport. The government, however, lacked the capacity to produce passports in sufficient numbers to meet demand and prioritized providing passports to those individuals who could demonstrate imminent need to travel or who had strong government connections. Obtaining a passport was a time-consuming and difficult process for most persons.

Internally Displaced Persons

The April 4 gunfire and explosions in Brazzaville displaced more than 17,000 persons, who fled their neighborhoods for safer parts of the city. The government blamed the Ninja/Nsiloulou, a former rebel group from the 1997-2003 civil war. Their leader, Pastor Ntumi, denied responsibility, and many suspected that the entire operation may have been coordinated by elements of the government as a political distraction prior the Constitutional Court's declaration of final presidential election results and to perpetuate a climate of fear and intimidation to prevent protests. Churches in the neighborhood of Plateau de 15 Ans in Brazzaville hosted approximately 10,000 internally displaced persons (IDPs) for approximately one week. There were reports of military personnel robbing IDPs as they passed through checkpoints. Two women reportedly gave birth while displaced. On April 5, the government launched security operations in the Pool region outside of Brazzaville to search for Ntumi. During the operation thousands more in the Pool region were displaced from their homes (see section 1.g.).

Protection of Refugees

Access to Asylum: The law provides for the granting of asylum or refugee status, and the government has a system for providing protection to refugees but not asylum seekers. There are no laws recognizing asylum seekers nor any laws implementing the protections afforded in the 1951 Refugee Convention, to which the government is a signatory. During the year the country hosted 46,049 refugees, 4,134 asylum seekers, and 3,087 persons of concern.

The National Refugee Assistance Committee (CNAR), a joint committee under the Ministry of Social Affairs and Humanitarian Action, Ministry of Justice, and Ministry of Foreign Affairs, handled applications for refugee status. The CNAR received most of its operating budget from UNHCR.

According to UNHCR, the CNAR eligibility board processed 129 asylum cases during the year; seven cases were granted refugee status, three cases were put on hold for further processing, and 119 cases were denied refugee status. There were no cases processed by the appeal board during the year.

The country saw an influx of persons fleeing violence in the CAR beginning in 2012. According to UNHCR, as of October 1, the country hosted 29,304 CAR refugees and asylum seekers.

As of July 2015, the government stopped granting prima facie status to refugees fleeing from the CAR. During the year UNHCR registered 2,078 CAR asylum seekers, but the government did not register the asylum claims until August. With the support of UNHCR, the CNAR adopted an expedited procedure to process asylum requests. Since August 29, the government registered 240 asylum-seeking families from the CAR (560 individuals), none of which were processed by the government's eligibility board for refugee status.

Local integration for refugees in the country was particularly difficult due to the cost of acquiring a residence permit, 350,000 CFA francs ($600). UNHCR was not aware of any refugees who obtained a residency card or alternative status as of October 20.

Employment: The law does not address employment for refugees, but various government decrees prohibit foreigners, including refugees, from practicing small trade activities and working in the public transportation sector. Following the operation to expel undocumented migrants in 2014, police aggressively implemented these laws, resulting in sudden and mass unemployment of refugees.

According to UNHCR, on multiple occasions during the year, refugees in Brazzaville reported police arbitrarily confiscated items they were selling, such as eggs and fruit, under threat of arrest or demand for a bribe.

Several rural localities banned foreigners from continuing their farming activities. According to customary laws, property owners may require foreigners to pay an extra licensing fee to lease property or land.

In recent years anecdotal evidence suggested quotas and excessive work permit fees limited refugee employment opportunities in the formal sector. Authorities required refugees to obtain two-year work permits that cost approximately 150,000 CFA francs ($260), approximately equivalent to three months' salary.

Many refugees worked informally in the agriculture sector to obtain food. Some refugees farmed land that belonged to local nationals in exchange for a percentage of the harvest or a cash payment.

Access to Basic Services: In July UNHCR received reports from refugees that a local government authority in Likuala started a registration operation for all foreigners in the region, including refugees, requiring a payment of 500 CFA francs ($0.85) for documents that under law are free of charge. In July local authorities ceased the registration operation after complaints from the international community.

UNHCR-funded primary schooling was accessible to most refugees. During the academic year, primary schools enrolled 9,226 refugee children, including 4,489 girls. Authorities severely limited access to secondary and vocational education for refugees. Most secondary education teachers at such schools were refugees who either volunteered to teach or were paid by the parents of refugee children. There were 2,713 refugee children enrolled in secondary school, of whom 1,123 were girls.

Durable Solutions: As of September 27, the country hosted 9,030 Rwandan refugees, 53 percent of whom were born in the Republic of the Congo, including 753 children unable to obtain birth certificates. According to UNHCR, in 2004-15 the government repatriated 445 Rwandan refugees. Since January the government repatriated seven additional Rwandan refugees.

At a tripartite meeting in 2012, the governments of the Republic of the Congo and Rwanda, with UNHCR, agreed to invoke a cessation clause that would revoke the refugee status of Rwandans in the country beginning on June 30, 2013. As of that date, the agreement required Rwandan refugees to return to Rwanda, formalize their legal status in the Congo, or apply for refugee status based on individual claims due to particular circumstances. UNHCR reported that 4,029 Rwandans subject to the cessation clause filed exemption requests with the government. During the year the government completed determination interviews for all

Rwandan refugees living in Brazzaville and Kintele, an estimated 1,400, but as of December, it had not made a decision on their status.

Section 3. Freedom to Participate in the Political Process

The constitution and law provide citizens the ability to choose their government in free and fair elections held by secret ballot and based on universal and equal suffrage. Nevertheless, irregularities restricting this ability occurred in the 2009 presidential, 2012 legislative and 2014 local elections, October 2015 referendum, and the March 2016 presidential elections.

Elections and Political Participation

Recent Elections: Long-serving incumbent President Denis Sassou N'Guesso was declared winner of the March 20 presidential election in the first round with 60.29 percent of the vote, according to official figures published by the Constitutional Court on April 4. The court cited a 68.92 percent voter turnout among the more than two million eligible voters, with a 100 percent voter turnout in at least three regions. The Constitutional Court rejected a challenge filed by second-place candidate Parfait Kolelas on technical grounds. Throughout the election period, local and international observer groups and diplomatic missions reported widespread fraud and irregularities. Some observer groups deemed the elections free and fair, but observers from these groups later admitted the government underwrote their work.

On February 1, the interior minister issued a decree scheduling the official presidential campaign period to run from March 4 to March 18. Candidates were able to submit applications to run as president from February 5 to 25. Applicants were required to submit a medical certificate, and prospective candidates were required to pay a nonrefundable deposit of 25,000 CFA francs ($43).

The government enacted a few electoral reforms, such as an electoral commission with an independent budget and the use of a single ballot. On March 4, candidate Jean-Marie Michel Mokoko called for a delay of the vote, complaining that the electoral register was inadequate and the new electoral commission was not truly independent.

In advance of the election, the government limited international observation credentials for diplomatic mission to three staff per mission, in stark contrast to previous elections.

On March 20, election day, authorities banned the use of motor vehicles and cut internet, SMS, and cell phone service for 48 hours, with few exceptions. While authorities restored some services, a partial communication blackout lasted until March 26.

Also on election day, international observers witnessed a number of irregularities including: incorrect voter lists; inconsistency in ballot boxes; prefilled voting tally sheets for voter stations in Brazzaville; polling officials allowing and encouraging underage and multiple voting, and instructing voters to vote only for the incumbent; polling stations opening late, and without adequate supplies; polling officials refusing entry to accredited international observers; payments provided to voters to vote for certain candidates; lack of uniform enforcement of voter ID requirements; polling officials, at separate locations, loyal to either the incumbent president or opposition candidates, blocking entry to voters supporting opposing candidates; ruling party loyalists impersonating representatives of other candidates; not posting final vote tally sheets on the exterior wall of polling stations as required; burning ballots after the polling station count; and prohibiting observation at regional and national vote compilation centers.

The electoral law specified the deadline for filing any challenge as five days after the date of the announcement of provisional results. The legal texts did not specify calendar days or working days for filing challenges, resulting in confusion among opposition candidates over the actual deadline, particularly during a period when some communications means were still blocked, making it difficult to relay results outside the capital.

Thousands of persons were paid to attend and transported to propresidential rallies and voting stations using government resources, while opposition supporters faced intimidation and security restrictions on attending their rallies or in trying to vote, according to numerous eyewitness and media accounts.

<u>Political Parties and Political Participation</u>: Many of the opposition parties aligned with two major coalitions during the year, FROCAD and the IDC, to create a unified IDC-FROCAD coalition. Remaining parties allied with the presidential majority.

There were attempts to impede criticism of the government through arrests and routine disruption of political meetings. For example, on March 8, police used tear gas to disperse a crowd supporting presidential candidate Claudine Munari in

Pointe-Noire. On March 10, police blocked presidential candidate Andre Okombi Salissa and opposition platform president Charles Zacharie Bowao from leaving Brazzaville to travel to the northern city of Impfondo for campaign purposes. On the same day, police used tear gas to disperse a crowd that had gathered to see presidential candidate Parfait Kolelas in the St. Paul Parish in Dolisie. On March 17, police blocked Kolelas supporters in Brazzaville from attending a large campaign rally, despite the law not requiring permits for rallies during official political campaign seasons.

In the weeks leading up to, and after the March 20 election, police and other internal security service personnel arrested dozens of opposition candidates, their campaign officials, and supporters. For example, from March 25 to 31, police arrested several campaign officials of presidential candidates Mokoko and Okombi Salissa.

Participation of Women and Minorities: No laws limit women's or minorities' political participation as voters or candidates. Observers suggested cultural constraints might limit the number of women in government. Sexual harassment discouraged women's participation in political activities. There were 10 women in the 72-seat senate and 13 women in the 139-seat national assembly. There were eight women in the 38-member cabinet appointed on April 30.

In 2014 the president signed a law requiring that women make up 30 percent of each party's slate of candidates for local or legislative elections. The 2015 constitution granted parity for women in political positions and mandated the creation of a national advisory council for women, but it did not specify whether the promotion of parity related to pay, benefits, appointment to political positions, or other issues.

The political process excludes many indigenous persons. Reasons included their isolation in remote areas, lack of registration, cultural barriers, and stigmatization by the majority Bantu population (see section 6). For example, a local government official reported that during the October 2015 referendum, the voting booth in Sibiti, a rural city with many indigenous persons, was open for only 30 minutes, from 7:30-8:00 a.m. Because indigenous communities in outer villages must travel several hours to reach Sibiti, no one reportedly voted.

Section 4. Corruption and Lack of Transparency in Government

The law provides for criminal penalties for corruption by officials; however, the government did not implement the law effectively, and many officials engaged in corrupt practices with impunity, despite the president's call for an end to corruption in his inauguration speech April 16.

According to the World Bank's most recent Worldwide Governance Indicators, government corruption was a severe problem, although the bank and the International Monetary Fund noted the government continued anticorruption reforms.

There was a widespread perception of corruption throughout government, including misuse of revenues from the oil and forestry sectors. Some local and international organizations claimed some government officials, through bribes or other fraud, regularly diverted revenues from these sectors into private overseas accounts before officially declaring the remaining revenues.

Corruption: On April 22, French authorities seized two luxury apartments in Paris owned by First Lady Antoinette Sassou N'Guesso, the result of an investigation of ill-gotten gains first started in 2010. In February French authorities seized 15 luxury vehicles belonging to members of the Sassou family and in September 2015 seized a luxury property in France titled in the name of President Sassou's nephew. In August international media reported the president's son Denis-Christel N'Guesso sold exclusive mining rights to Australian mining company Sundance in exchange for 30 percent of profits, according to leaked internal company documents. Denis-Christel Sassou N'Guesso denied involvement.

Financial Disclosure: The constitution mandates that senior elected or appointed officials disclose their financial interests and holdings both before taking office and upon leaving office. Failure to do so is legal grounds for dismissal from a senior position. The Constitutional Court is tasked with enforcement of this constitutional provision; however, authorities did not enforce this provision, and no financial disclosure statements were made public during the year. One official noted that disclosure of assets could lead to attacks on personal property of elected officials by opposition supporters as occurred prior to the referendum. The autonomous agency National Agency for Financial Investigation (ANIF) is tasked with investigating suspicious financial transactions and, if necessary, forwarding the information to competent judicial authorities. Its mandate is primarily related to the fight against money laundering and transnational criminal groups; however, ANIF's mandate extends to transactions by government officials as well.

<u>Public Access to Information</u>: The constitution and law provide for public access to government information for citizens, noncitizens, and the foreign media; however, authorities did not effectively implement the law. Processing fees were nominal for requests for information, although there were generally lengthy delays before the government released information, if at all. Individuals may appeal denials of access to information to the Constitutional Court, but the court did not hear denial appeals.

Section 5. Governmental Attitude Regarding International and Nongovernmental Investigation of Alleged Violations of Human Rights

A number of domestic and international human rights groups occasionally operated without government restriction during their investigations and when publishing their findings on human rights cases. Government officials were no more cooperative with and responsive to international groups than with domestic human rights groups. Some domestic human rights groups tended not to report on specific incidents due to fear of reprisal by the government, while others were denied access or permission to perform assessments.

For example, several local human rights organizations were denied access to conduct humanitarian assessment missions in the Pool region after the government initiated security operations in response to April 4 violence in Brazzaville. Following election-related violence, authorities refused human rights NGOs and journalists' entry to morgues normally open to the public.

On February 26, security officials refused entry to Amnesty International's deputy regional director for West and Central Africa despite his having a valid visa, invitation letter, and confirmations of meetings with authorities. Officials confiscated his passport and held him overnight at the airport in Brazzaville before expelling him the following day to Dakar.

Other international human rights organizations that requested access to the region, such as U.K.-based Amnesty International, and French-based International Federation for Human Rights, were denied. On April 19, the minister of communication and a government spokesperson told reporters that access to the Pool region had been denied to organizations whose aim was to "criticize national authorities and conduct biased and one-sided investigations."

<u>The United Nations or Other International Bodies</u>: In April the government initially delayed approval of a request for access to the Pool region by a UN

humanitarian assessment team. In May, UN Secretary-General Ban Ki-Moon urged President Sassou to "ensure that humanitarian and other relevant actors are granted access to the affected areas." From June 7 to 11, the government permitted access to the UN assessment team, arranging for it to work with a team from the Ministry of Social Affairs and Humanitarian Action.

Government Human Rights Bodies: The government-sponsored HRC is charged with acting as a government watchdog and addressing public concerns on human rights problems. Some civil society members claimed the commission was completely ineffective, lacked independence, was primarily composed of persons who had no expertise in human rights, and was created to appease the international community. The president appointed most, if not all, of its members. The president of the commission, Jean Martin Mbemba, was the subject of a long-running political crime trial, but authorities permitted him to leave the country in 2014 to undergo medical treatment in France. The vice president of the commission, Maurice Massengo Tiasse, fled into hiding for several days in October 2015 after police raided his independent radio station, and he subsequently fled the country. On October 12, following his filing a human rights report with the UN Human Rights Council in Geneva, the government issued an international arrest warrant for Tiasse for illegal possession of state weapons and ammunition and endangering the security of the state.

The HRC did not undertake any activities directly responding to human rights problems in the country during the year.

Section 6. Discrimination, Societal Abuses, and Trafficking in Persons

Women

Rape and Domestic Violence: Rape is illegal, but the government did not effectively enforce the law. The law prescribes five to 10 years in prison for violators. According to a local women's group, however, penalties actually imposed for rape ranged from as few as several months' imprisonment to rarely more than three years. NGOs and women's advocacy groups reported rape, especially spousal rape, was common. A local NGO noted 332 rapes reported in the first nine months of the year, adding that this figure likely represented only a small fraction of rapes actually committed. The cost to obtain a police report verifying rape was 30,000 CFA francs ($50). Authorities prosecuted fewer than 25 percent of reported rapes, according to local and international NGOs. According to the Association for Progressive Communications, a regional NGO, medical rape kits were available only in Brazzaville. In Pointe-Noire, only HIV tests were free for rape victims; all other laboratory tests were at the expense of the patient.

Domestic violence against women, including rape and beatings, was widespread but rarely reported. There were no specific provisions in the law outlawing spousal battery other than general statutes prohibiting assault. The extended family or village traditionally dealt with domestic violence matters, and victims reported only more extreme incidents to police because of victims' fears of social stigma and retaliation and a lack of confidence in the courts. Local NGOs sponsored domestic violence awareness campaigns and workshops.

Sexual Harassment: Sexual harassment is illegal. Generally, the penalty is two to five years in prison. In particularly egregious cases, the penalty may equal the 10-year prison sentence maximum for rape. The government did not effectively enforce these laws. No official statistics were available, but according to local NGOs, sexual harassment was very common but rarely reported. Sexual harassment discouraged women's participation in political, economic, and social activities.

According to women's rights activists and students at Marien Ngouabi University, professors systematically sexually harassed female students, demanding sexual favors in return for good grades and recommendations.

Reproductive Rights: Couples and individuals have the right to decide the number, spacing, and timing of their children, free from discrimination, coercion, or violence, but often lacked the information and means to do so. Emergency health care normally was not provided for abortion, since most of the population believed it to be illegal, and abortion is not allowed in public hospitals (there are no private hospitals). There are no restrictions on the right to access contraceptives. NGOs and individuals reported that a previously funded government program to make available male and female contraceptives free of charge as part of anti-HIV and AIDS efforts had received no funding and was discontinued. The UN Population Division estimated 20.7 percent of girls and women ages 15 to 45 used a modern method of contraception in 2015. In 2015 a joint assessment by the World Bank and several UN organizations, including the World Health Organization, estimated there were 442 maternal deaths per 100,000 live births (up from 410 per 100,000 in 2013).

During the year NGOs reported local health clinics and public hospitals were generally in poor condition and lacked experienced health-care staff. For example, in the rural villages outside Sibiti, there were five medical clinics serving five villages, none of which had a doctor on staff. Women desiring to give birth at a hospital with skilled attendants had to travel three hours to the closest hospital located in Sibiti. According to a local government official, women sometimes died in labor on the way to the hospital. Women from both the indigenous and other rural communities suffered disproportionate rates of fistula due to unattended childbirth and rape. Despite the law mandating free emergency obstetric care and Caesarian sections, women had to provide their own medical equipment for doctors to use during the operations, which cost 100,000 CFA francs ($170).

Discrimination: Both customary marriage and family laws and civil laws enacted by the government govern the rights of women, children, and extended families. Adultery is illegal for both women and men, although the penalty differs. Under civil law the husband can receive only a fine for adultery, while the wife can receive a prison sentence. A man committing adultery with a married woman can receive the same prison sentence as the adulterous woman in addition to a fine. For marriages celebrated under local custom, the penalties do not apply except in cases where customary polygyny is specifically renounced or by a subsequent civil marriage. Polygyny is legal, while polyandry is not. The family code divides a husband's estate among a surviving spouse, children, and extended family.

Women experienced discrimination in divorce settlements, especially in regard to retaining property and financial assets. According to a local NGO, widows often were not accorded their legal rights of land and property inheritance. The law limits bride wealth to a symbolic amount of 50,000 CFA francs (S85), although families negotiated much higher amounts.

By law men are considered the head of the household, unless the father becomes incapacitated or abandons the family. The law dictates that in the absence of an agreement between spouses, men shall choose the residence of the family.

Women experienced economic discrimination with respect to employment, credit, equal pay, and owning or managing businesses. Access to education and wage employment continued to improve slowly for women, particularly in urban areas. A few local and international NGOs had microcredit programs for women, and government ministries, including those of social affairs and agriculture, helped women create small income-producing businesses.

Children

<u>Birth Registration</u>: Children acquire citizenship from their parents. Birth within the territory of the country does not automatically confer citizenship, although exceptions exist for children born of missing or stateless parents, or children born of foreign parents, at least one of whom was also born in the Congo. The government does not require registration of births; it is up to parents to request birth registration for a child. A birth certificate is necessary, however, for school enrollment and other services. Indigenous people, particularly those living in remote villages, had difficulty registering, since registration offices were located only in district and provincial capitals.

<u>Education</u>: Education is compulsory, tuition-free, and universal until age 16, but families are required to pay for books, uniforms, and health insurance fees. School enrollment was generally higher in urban areas. Specific data were lacking, but most indigenous children could not attend school because they did not have birth certificates or could not afford the 1,200 CFA francs ($2) per month insurance fee. School facilities were overcrowded and poorly maintained, especially in rural areas. Girls and boys attended primary school in approximately equal numbers; however, boys were five times more likely than girls to go to high school and four times more likely than girls in high school to go to a university.

<u>Child Abuse</u>: Child abuse was not commonly reported to authorities, but NGOs reported it was prevalent.

<u>Early and Forced Marriage</u>: The law prohibits child marriage, and the legal age for marriage is 18 years for women and 21 for men. Underage marriage is possible with a judge's permission and with the permission of both sets of parents; the law does not specify a minimum age in such a case. In practice many couples engaged in an informal common-law marriage not legally recognized, while grooms saved for a legally recognized traditional, court, or church wedding. According to the UN Population Fund, 33 percent of women 20 to 24 years old were married by the age of 18 in 2009, although the government expressed skepticism that the percentage was so high.

There was no government program focused on preventing early or forced marriage. The penalty for forced marriage between an adult and child is a prison sentence of three months to two years and a fine of 150,000 to 1.5 million CFA francs ($255 to $2,555).

<u>Sexual Exploitation of Children</u>: A child protection code provides penalties for crimes against children such as trafficking, pornography, neglect, and abuse.

Penalties for these crimes range from forced labor to fines of up to 10 million CFA francs ($17,123) and prison sentences of several years. The penalty for child pornography includes a prison sentence of up to one year and a fine up to 500,000 CFA francs ($856). The minimum age for consensual sex is 18. The maximum penalty for sex with a minor is five years' imprisonment and a fine of 10 million CFA francs ($17,035). The government appointed special judges to hear cases pertaining to children at the Court of Appeals, but the court heard no cases during the year. A lack of specificity in the child protection code was an obstacle to successful prosecution.

There were cases of children, particularly those who lived on the streets in the larger cities, subjected to sexual exploitation. Authorities increasingly enforced laws that prohibit the exploitation of children, including sexual exploitation. A 2013 study by the International Organization for Migration indicated the majority of children subjected to commercial sexual exploitation originated in the DRC. The extent of sex trafficking and exploitation of children in rural areas remained unclear.

Displaced Children: During April there were large numbers of internally displaced children in Brazzaville as well as the southern Pool region due to insecurity from attacks and security operations (see section 1 g.). International organizations assisted with programs to feed and shelter street children, the majority of whom lived in Brazzaville and Pointe-Noire and were believed to be from the DRC. Many begged, while others sold cheap or stolen goods to support themselves.

International Child Abductions: The country is not a party to the 1980 Hague Convention on the Civil Aspects of International Child Abduction. See the Department of State's *Annual Report on International Parental Child Abduction* at travel.state.gov/content/childabduction/en/legal/compliance.html.

Anti-Semitism

There was a very small Jewish community. There were no known reports of anti-Semitic acts.

Trafficking in Persons

See the Department of State's annual *Trafficking in Persons Report* at www.state.gov/j/tip/rls/tiprpt/.

Persons with Disabilities

The law specifically prohibits discrimination against persons with physical, sensory, intellectual, and mental disabilities in employment, education, access to health care, or in the provision of other state services, including the justice system. The Ministry of Social Affairs and Humanitarian Action is the lead ministry responsible for protecting the rights of persons with disabilities. In 2009 the ministry introduced a national plan to provide access for persons with disabilities, and the ministry's 2013-16 Social Plan of Action includes an eight-point plan for improving the lives of such persons. There are no laws, however, mandating access for persons with disabilities. The government did not take action during the year to provide equal access for persons with disabilities to public spaces or transportation. The government provides special schools for students with hearing disabilities in Brazzaville and Pointe-Noire. The government mainstreamed children with vision disabilities and children with physical disabilities into regular public schools. In 2014 the government started a school to train social workers, teachers for children with disabilities, and sign language instructors.

National/Racial/Ethnic Minorities

The law prohibits discrimination based on ethnicity. Regional ethnic discrimination existed, but it was not as prevalent as in the years following the civil war that ended in 2003, which divided the country largely along regional and ethnic lines. Discrimination was not evident in private-sector hiring and buying patterns or in the provision of government services such as education, health, or housing. There were no episodes of regional or ethnic violence reported during the year. The perception of regional and ethnic bias was most acute in the upper echelons of government. Although the relationships among ethnic, regional, and political equities could be difficult to discern due to substantial intermarriage and increased geographic mobility over recent generations, a large portion of the general officer corps consisted of individuals from the northern departments.

Indigenous People

According to UN Children's Fund and local NGOs, indigenous people throughout the country, in both remote and urban areas, were severely marginalized with regard to employment, health services, housing, and education, in part due to their geographic isolation and different cultural norms. Many indigenous people in remote areas were not aware of the concept of voting and had minimal ability to influence government decisions affecting their interests, despite government claims of high voter registration and participation in the presidential election. Other indigenous communities living in more-urban areas understood the concept of political participation but feared harassment by members of the Bantu population for participation and lacked access to travel to voting booths.

Indigenous communities living among the majority Bantu populations lived in substandard housing on the perimeters of villages. A community activist reported that beatings and killings of indigenous people by Bantus were common in rural areas. Bantus often forced indigenous people to work in their fields for little to no pay and refused to purchase food from indigenous vendors. A government official reported that indigenous women and girls suffered from gender-based violence, and teenage pregnancy among indigenous girls was common. Bantu men often impregnated indigenous girls and later denied paternity, offering no child support. Indigenous women suffered from a disproportionate rate of fistulas resulting from unattended childbirth and rape.

A local authority reported that logging activity had displaced both forest dwelling communities and wildlife on which they depended.

A 2011 law provides special status and recognition for indigenous populations. Additionally, Article 16 of the 2015 constitution stipulates the state shall provide promotion and protection of indigenous peoples' rights. The government did not implement these laws.

Acts of Violence, Discrimination, and Other Abuses Based on Sexual Orientation and Gender Identity

There is no law that specifically prohibits consensual same-sex sexual conduct. The penal code prescribes imprisonment of three months to two years and a fine for those who commit a "public outrage against decency." The law prescribes a punishment of six months to three years and a fine for anyone who "commits a shameless act or an act against nature with an individual of the same sex under the age of 21." Authorities did not invoke the law to arrest or prosecute lesbian, gay, bisexual, transgender, or intersex (LGBTI) persons. On occasion, however, police officers harassed gay men and claimed the law prohibited same-sex sexual activity to elicit a small bribe. There are no laws that limit freedom of speech or assembly specifically for LGBTI persons.

The Association in Support of Vulnerable Groups, a gay rights NGO, sits on the National HIV/AIDS Committee, whose meetings the president or the minister of health chairs. A second organization, Arc de Ciel, represents the interests of gay homeless youth in Brazzaville. There was no known advocacy group to represent the interests of LGBTI individuals in the country.

There were no known cases of violence against LGBTI individuals during the year. Although at the official level authorities did not discriminate against LGBTI persons, gay men, particularly the young and the poor, reportedly were vulnerable.

HIV and AIDS Social Stigma

Public opinion polls conducted by the World Bank in 2012 showed significant societal discrimination against individuals with HIV/AIDS. The law provides penalties for unlawful divulgence of medical records by practitioners, negligence in treatment by health-care professionals, family abandonment, and unwarranted termination of employment. Civil society organizations advocating for the rights of persons with HIV/AIDS were fairly well organized and sought fair treatment, especially regarding employment.

Other Societal Violence or Discrimination

After the government launched security operations in the Pool region in April, there were more than 20 incidents of highway robbery and carjacking in the region, largely populated by Lari people. Many of these incidents involved violence, and there were confirmed cases of rape, shooting, beating, and stabbing.

Section 7. Worker Rights

a. Freedom of Association and the Right to Collective Bargaining

The law provides for the right of workers--except members of the security forces and other services "essential for protecting the general interest," including members of the armed forces, police, gendarmerie, and some personnel at ports and airports--to form and join unions of their choice without previous authorization or excessive requirements. The law allows unions to conduct their activities without interference.

Workers have the right to strike, provided they have exhausted all lengthy and complex conciliation and nonbinding arbitration procedures and given due notice. Participation in an unlawful strike constitutes serious misconduct and can result in criminal prosecution. The law requires the continuation of a minimum service in all public services as essential to protect the general interest. A minimum service requirement binds workers in essential services to a limit on the length of time they may strike. The employer determines the extent of the minimum service without negotiating with the parties to the dispute. Refusal to take part in providing the minimum service during strikes is considered gross misconduct. There were no known cases of workers in these essential services being terminated for violating the minimum service rule, likely due to the cumbersome termination process for civil servants. Instead, employers either transferred some workers who violated the rule to another service or denied them some job privileges.

The law provides for the right to bargain collectively. The law prohibits antiunion discrimination and requires the reinstatement of workers dismissed for union activity. The government generally did not effectively enforce applicable laws. Resources, inspections, and remediation were inadequate. There are no penalties for violations.

Freedom of association and the right to collective bargaining were not always respected. Most unions were reportedly weak and subject to government influence due to corruption. As a result, in cases where demonstrations would run counter to the government's interest, the government persuaded union leaders to prevent workers from demonstrating.

A dialogue continued between unions and the government on labor problems, such as basic salary scales and bonus structures. Salary increases for unionized state workers promised by the government as part of the dialogue in 2013 had yet to materialize for some categories of government employees.

There were reports employers used hiring practices such as subcontracting and short-term contracts to circumvent laws prohibiting antiunion discrimination.

b. Prohibition of Forced or Compulsory Labor

The constitution prohibits forced or compulsory labor unless imposed pursuant to a criminal penalty lawfully mandated by a court. The law, however, allows persons to be requisitioned for work of public interest and provides for their possible imprisonment if they refuse.

The law prohibits the forcible or fraudulent abduction of persons, including young persons under 18, and imposes penalties for these criminal offenses.

The government took steps to prevent and eliminate forced labor, but only relating to trafficked persons. Beginning in 2012 the government worked with the UN Office on Drugs and Crime and a foreign partner to initiate a three-year program to train personnel on and draft complete trafficking-in-persons legislation that would include both adults and children. The bill awaited cabinet and parliamentary review before promulgation.

The indigenous population was especially vulnerable to forced labor in the agricultural sector. In September indigenous rights activists in the southern cities of Sibiti and Dolisie reported that the majority population, called Bantus, often forced indigenous people to harvest manioc and other crops without pay and under the threat of physical abuse or death.

Also see the Department of State's annual *Trafficking in Persons Report* at www.state.gov/j/tip/rls/tiprpt/.

c. Prohibition of Child Labor and Minimum Age for Employment

By law children under age 16 may not be employed, even as apprentices, without a waiver from the minister of national education. The law prohibits the following crimes against all children up to age 18: forced labor, trafficking and all forms of slavery; child soldiering and forced recruitment for child soldiering; prostitution; the use, procuring, or offering of a child for the production of pornography or for pornographic performances; and the use of children by an adult for illegal activities.

The law includes specific ranges of penalties for violators of the worst forms of child labor. The maximum penalties for many of the most serious violations are 1.16 million CFA francs ($1,975) or five years in prison. According to a local antihuman-trafficking NGO and representatives from the Ministry of Social Affairs and Humanitarian Action, the lack of capacity to prosecute offenders in the judicial system made possible penalties even less of a deterrent. Violators did not fear prosecution.

The Ministry of Labor, which is responsible for enforcing child labor laws, concentrated its limited resources on the formal wage sector. Data on the number of children removed from child labor were not available, although the ministry reported authorities aided an NGO's efforts to rescue 10 children from trafficking. International aid groups reported little change in child labor conditions.

Although there are laws and policies designed to protect children from exploitation in the workplace, child labor was a problem in the informal sector. Children, including children from Benin and the DRC, were subjected to domestic servitude, market vending, and forced agricultural and fishing work. Child victims experienced harsh treatment, long work hours, and almost no access to education or health services. Additionally, they received little or no remuneration for their work. There were no official government statistics on general child labor.

Children as young as six, especially indigenous children in rural areas, often worked long hours in the fields harvesting cassava and carrying heavy loads of firewood. A local authority reported this was considered culturally acceptable, although not officially legal.

Also see the Department of Labor's *Findings on the Worst Forms of Child Labor* at www.dol.gov/ilab/reports/child-labor/findings/.

d. Discrimination with Respect to Employment and Occupation

The constitution and law prohibit discrimination based on family background, ethnicity, social condition, age, political or philosophical beliefs, gender, religion, region of origin within the country, place of residence in the country, language, HIV-positive status, or disability. The constitution and law do not specifically prohibit discrimination against persons based on national origin or citizenship, sexual orientation or gender identity, or having communicable diseases other than HIV. The government did not effectively enforce these prohibitions. Labor law does not specifically reiterate these antidiscrimination provisions. Discrimination in employment and occupation sometimes occurred with respect to women, refugees, and indigenous people. While the law prohibits discrimination based on gender and stipulates women have the right to equal pay for equal work, women were underrepresented in the formal sector of the economy. Most women worked in the informal sector and thus had little or no access to employment benefits. Women in rural areas were especially disadvantaged in terms of education and wage employment, and they were confined largely to family farming, small-scale commerce, and child-rearing responsibilities.

e. Acceptable Conditions of Work

The national minimum wage was 90,000 CFA francs ($153) per month in the formal sector. There was no official minimum wage for the agricultural and other informal sectors. High urban prices and dependent extended families obliged many workers, including teachers and health-care workers, to seek secondary employment, mainly in the informal sector.

The law provides for a standard workweek of seven hours per day with a one-hour lunch break, five days a week. There was no legal limit on the number of hours worked per week, and the law provides for paid annual holidays and four months of maternity leave. The law stipulates overtime pay for all work in excess of regular working hours. For public-sector workers, this is 35 hours per week. In private companies, overtime is any work beyond the business' normal working hours (usually 40 to 42 hours per week). There is no legal prohibition of excessive compulsory overtime. Overtime is subject to agreement between employer and employee. Employers generally observed these standards, and employers usually paid workers in cash for overtime work.

Although health and safety regulations require biannual visits to businesses by inspectors from the Ministry of Labor, such visits occurred much less frequently, and enforcement of findings was uneven. The Ministry of Labor employed 12 full-time inspectors responsible only for inspecting the formal sector, which was insufficient to enforce compliance with labor laws. Unions generally were vigilant in calling attention to dangerous working conditions; however, the observance of safety standards often was lax in both the private and public sectors. Workers have no specific right to remove themselves from situations that endanger their health or safety without jeopardizing their employment. There were no exceptions for foreign or migrant workers. According to NGOs, labor violations were common in commercial fishing and logging operations, rock quarries, and private construction sites. Authorities did not effectively protect employees in these situations.